.

Folktales and Elegies

poems by

Sal Ragen

Finishing Line Press
Georgetown, Kentucky

Folktales and Elegies

ACKNOWLEDGMENTS

I'd like to thank *The Dogwood Journal of Poetry and Prose, Allegory Ridge,*
and the *River Heron Review* for publishing "Pizza and Steakhouse Stars,"
"Memorial Day," and "Gills, 1992," respectively.
Thank you to *Pine Row Press* for publishing "A Self-Contained Plane of
Existence," to *The MacGuffin* for publishing "Cattywampus," and "Two
Soldiers."
Thank you to *Spectrum Literary Journal* for publishing, "Abyssina," and
"Sassie."

Thank you to Dr. Adrian Anast and Gordon Mennenga for their early
kindness and sincere encouragement that strengthened my spirit to keep
writing. Thank you to the University of Nebraska-Omaha's MFA Writing
Program and director Kevin Clouther and all the mentors for the oustanding
instruction, guidance, and encouragement. Thank you to Jessica Hendry
Nelson for her mentorship.
Thank you to my husband Ronnie Ragen Jr. aka Pa for his love and support.
Thank you to the Almighty for everything.

Publisher: Leah Huete de Maines
Editor: Christen Kincaid
Cover Art: Sal Ragen
Author Photo: Sal Ragen
Cover Design: Elizabeth Maines McCleavy

Order online: www.finishinglinepress.com
also available on amazon.com

Author inquiries and mail orders:
Finishing Line Press
PO Box 1626
Georgetown, Kentucky 40324
USA

Contents

for my Babushka

WORDS

I, the ONE, moved around in the invisible things
like the sun from east to west and from west to east.

Sun comes up home here
across a withered bean field
down over raggy tops of cedars
way back in the timber and sets
even in the hard hells of winter
it's the song that never ends.

Time moves funny here too
as sound does in the nighttime
my limited corporeal self
all realities are tricksters.
It's best to take a nip or two
if you have it

calm the jitters
grease the wheels

old joints gain courage
only works for ten minutes
unless you drown
might scare off the booger-men
between those glassy prisms

Advice: that's old hat to everyone
but them, those boogies
end up the sad unemployed

my abomination
those pre-dream memories

Granny and Pappy
I walk   in
He is making gravy
she hollers out "get in here, sister."

it slices open my trout gut
entrails and shit
You see, I found my grieving self.

then and now aches and pains
right words wrong words
sloth self move like that
tender not seen
forty years of   it didn't work.

It's the giant suck of lostness.
no childhood, some childhood
my child all grown

I pretend not to see   what's next

my dog Lee
house burning crumpled up
in a ditch grave
Egypt my black cat slipped away

Then he
Then the words

Pappy said if
you ever fall out of the boat
into the river
let the current take you down,
ride it under the dark
hold tight let it raze at your limbs
the dark will pop you back up.

so, it's a story.

salvation comes as salvation does
in the change, in the equinox

I write when cotton seeds blow
my little bantys peck the dirt
ideas are light as pixies riding
white fluff catching
sail through my backyard
and hayfield out yonder.

ideas tall as cottonwoods
which are notorious
for lightning strikes
in thunderstorms.
beacons for the flame
gunned down in glory
by a lightning bolt

a good way to go

                just a thought
                fall in and let it go
                burn up bright
                hold life
                while it's still moving
                wave at the hellions
                black dog obits
                passing by in buicks
                wave flags
                fuck it to those
                just want to fight
                all the damn time.

my curtain
goes like this

        I will be held together in darkness under his wings.

no words
then new words.

Thus, he goes through a cycle, and he goes down and he rises up across the sky and beneath the earth with the light of his rays. And he was there, on the track unceasingly.

(from The Second Book of Enoch)

VAN BUREN COUNTY ROADS

granny called them indian paintbrushes. i rarely went and saw her when she was dying. her face had changed. her eyes were dollish and wide. i didn't know her. she stopped talking. instead, she moaned into corners of rooms. those doll eyes held tear pools. i could see in the mirror. we both had changed.

last i saw her she walked through me. i was not there. maybe she was. that was true in another way. delayed and way deep in the dna the grief was passed to me. i feel the flowers tickling the back of my bare legs—going straight for my spine, pushing my shoulders over farther. i buckle under the weight of the indian paintbrushes. the pink welts, me rubbing spit on my arms and legs.

its the goddamnest thing, really–cemeteries. she is there or supposed to be. she's not. but on the drive all these county roads branching out there is a constant echo of her thick german, hope, north dakota accent talking to my eleven-year-old self. she'll stop red omni, get out and have her navy polyester pants rolled into her chore boots, fanny up in the air picking purple wildflowers to bring home with her. never mind the peanut gallery in pickups or faceless amish peeking out their buggies at us.

here's something she never said. grief isn't crying and sleeping. it ain't about wearing black armbands, covering mirrors, casseroles. it's things that cannot be photographed. the tiniest parts of people stay too long. it's not them, right? they are gone. i've made my own ghosts of torment. this will kill me quicker and faster than alcohol or the angel of death himself. but it's a fault line in the heart that never heals–that kind of slow death akin to suicide if you tend to blame love for everything wrong in the world. for me, it's the wildflowers.

DECEMBER 30

thirty years of body lean into the western sun. my cheek to a cold window pane. my finger holds the place of a single star crossed out. an ache of old, my friend, a curse of hope lost and found again. we drink wine from the cup of a children's god. we find a crack in the wall small enough to squeeze through. we see clouds where they drip down into snow tracks. we hold a simple peace like warm soup on those days when the cold hides in bones.

we stare into a strange funeral for a year gone by. we dream of antebellum and watch the hard heels of flaming men pulling, pushing, and flattening the planes. then it's grandfather clocks covered in black tablecloths. the only luminary left had died. then we are still like space without sound. my friend carries me against his breast and under his wing. we fly across dark pastures. he shows me a boy holding a lantern walking cows down a gravel road. a beloved born from the fern frost and ice flowers of our window.

THE GIRL REFUSES TO DIE

she crawled from her freshwater mollusk, winged, spiked, and turtlebacked. gritty eyes, sand scratching, everywhere, sand in her teeth, bleeding gums, stuck to skin between boney fingers. four hours flat, compressed by sounds, ceiling vibrations, deflated draped into flooded alleyways. harelipped, fried, and singed when the sun stopped at noon for days. crawling out from the three ridge mucket mausoleum gave her spinsters, those social call clocks for adornment, sinking in washboard bottom pearls. giving up hundreds of years and crawling back inside herself, she gained more than just ghost stories. calloused hands and feet moved more battleground. this wasn't about him—his scars made her transient years ago.

this is a reincarnate revolving propeller ride, knees graveling, stumbling by silver cord. slicing cuts and green bruises. if she keeps coming back—waving the second death it will be blunt force trauma incurring debt for each injury in cycle currents. faith and fall are hope in the black. curtain parts when she presents the old skin suit to the stage with the rest of them. ecclesiastes since time and from the bowl of her shell to a cleft deep inside the mother terra rossa, she is nothing but mirrors in the underwater limestone. reaching, she pines the hiraeth in the challenger deep. returning, she fades the grave.

GILLS, 1992

minty prayed to be swallowed by a giant catfish. then she jumped from the savanna-sabula bridge into the mississippi river. it was just the right orison, the catfish would later tell her.

leroy, a big fan of hamlet, came up through a slip in the bosky dells. a sorrel flathead born in 1922, and three times the size of an s-10 pickup truck. he was a shovelhead, a yellow pied pylodictis olivaris cousin to the river-rat. he had old hook marks, scarred over scratches, and his whisker barbs half missing. teeny tiny suckerfish stuck to his yellow belly mosaic. he amassed eagle claw hooks, red jigs and rigs, booyah spinnerbaits and lead sinkers. minty was impressed by the finery of it all.

getting swallowed by a giant catfish isn't as complicated as it sounds. in she went, fanny on a pink slip-n-slide. kind salutations and such exchanges, one fish and one girl. minty shared a meal with leroy: cicadas, bloated perch, and royal mulberries. she relaxed on leroy's swim bladder no different than a warm waterbed. she stayed up all night riding the sway and untangling fishing line. she reckoned she was tired of folks being so damn mean all the time. they're bastards really, even when they're not. there's only so much an empath can absorb and excrete. expect death by impaction. akin to a bloody fecal gut bomb.

she wondered about jonah, his deaf messages, a bit harsh in that he wanted nineveh nepalmed. she had no desire for that business. she would stay put with her totem and keep house for wayfarying, vittles and dibs on tiny divers. she'd preserve: bream, snails, crawdads, minnows, sunnies, small perch and shad. she'd keep the gills clean she'd help dig the trench nest for spawning season. once the gal dropped off the eggs, she would love on them and help protect them. minty told leroy she was never going back to helly trailer court—she sent her au revoirs. he offered her 2,340 miles of river for roaming, including his hometown of Orleans with it's loud underwater jazz. it was an indefinite abysm two hundred feet deep, a world just for transcendental punchy types.

theirs was an unspoken tenderness. so naturally, they were boot and rally from the get-go. leroy loved to scare the hell out of river divers and yokel noodlers. he loved to talk about how water was a conscious organism, that it's an artist binding life into one universal network of energy, and she never tired of hearing it. no finis, no carcass, no tearing the veil over and again. it was a rare quietus per Hamlet, leroy said. minty spared him the caterwauling dirges. her only regret came in the form of certain memories. hankering for ham and biscuits, shooting watermelons, and earning granny's black licorice candy for not blaspheming. even in the still, everything happened as it was supposed to. the curtain drop was a sweet by and by: a simple fare-thee-well, fare-thee-well. the rest–really was silence.

ABYSSINIA

Great Aunt Irene bought a bus ticket for the girl she called Beans on a bus northeast to Fair Day, Missouri. Beans was a tall twelve-year-old dressed in silver sequins that shed its glitter bits everywhere the girl walked. Beans or Miss Josephine Mitchel Carter believed in the booger man but was not afraid of him. Great Aunt Irene did not and encouraged her to give, give, give if she want anything like a decent meal of meat and potatoes and a half-assed roof over her head. Beans disagreed and was on her own from there.

She sat next to a young man that had a death grip on a cardboard sign that read Chicago or Bust. His little red lips spoke French and smelled like fruit punch and gin. He spoke smoke rings and mouthed words at those walking by them while they hit his elbow with their hat boxes and carpetbags. She knew they would part at some point and her heart broke long before he stood up to leave. When he did he held out his hand. She reached out and held it for a few moments. Then the bus driver yelled him off the line.

Fair Day, Missouri came and went with a shrug of the shoulders. She dumped her old life in a burn barrel near a diner. She was walking free in a pair of shorts and she felt inspired to a bit of wickedness. So she stole a pair of overalls and a brown jacket off a clothesline. Later in the day, Beans pulled weeds for a slice of peach pie in a hamlet of red oaks and crackerbox houses. Then gabbers gabbed and it wasn't long and old folks carried cookies and pies to her and she pulled their crabgrass, purslane, lambs quarters, chickweed, and creeping charlie. They almost had her reformed, pressed into a dress, and adopted but she snuck out during their afternoon nap.

In town, she met a back alley kitchen inventor of nothing, a serial salesman who bought her coffee and a roll when she wasn't hungry. He played kindness very well but the truth shot out his eyes like scared frogs. Then he got a little handsy but he had underestimated his prey and received his own date with the dirt. His obit would read beloved son and devoted father. She found a creek and celebrated. Without any kind of pomp or circumstance, the Almighty came down and helped her wash the blood off.

It turned out, he also had a knack for making quarters appear in the mouth of perch. She cooked the fish over a small fire and ate with him. Then he sent her on her way to buy new duds.

The small town's soup line stretched out half a mile and she watched a yellow pug run the line and growl at folks. A whistle sailed through the air and the pug stopped at an ancient shortie she came to know as "Silk." The pug was official and his title was Sissy's Conrad Wallis. Campfire news about this four-legged democrat made the coastlines in less than a week. The pug had news stories sketched on the walls of train cars. Little Wallis had made out the First National Bank of St. Germain's with unmarked dollar bills folded in his red hankerchief collar.

Silk caught sight of the girl walking toward the line. The pug ran after and yipped, "stop!" After a second or two of standing there and looking over one another, they all silently decided and were boot and rally from there. When they did talk it was always campfire quiet and away from the railmen.

Silk Rasmussen, Fourth Generation Boog of Borney Oaks, was a seventy-year-old southern gentleman, and a small legend from an old town in Wisconsin. Silk had a habit of welding himself to union jobs then scab, and then union again. Every day somebody else. Every night some other story. Over their journey, he carved out his will and testament on an apple tree in Nebraska. *Beans to Inherit Sissy's Conrad Wallis immediately upon death, Silk R.*

Go do everything, he told her. Everything but carnivals. Facts of life as he saw them came while they picked Moonglow, Luscious, and Seckel varieties. It was a small manageable gang. Their train cars flew over landscapes of blue snow and fir trees miles deep. Mornings came with pug breath, apple peels, and bird wings made from playing cards. Silk sang about cigarette trees and hens laying soft-boiled eggs. Beans like to mail out random postcards to imaginary addresses. *Dear Old Matilda*, she wrote. *Tis another hard left to San Fran bound with coal. Are you supposing on Christmas? If so, I'll be there with bells on. Abyssinia, Beans.*

It was nearly winter when Silk rose up before the cookie began burning the bacon. He loaded baskets and trucks in a hurry. This was the last season in view for the old man from everywhere yet nowhere who got saved, baptized, and resurrected at the last minute in a frog pond. He gave away his pocket treasures, picked apples in record numbers, and sang songs no one had heard before. Silk's last words were, "He's a pug, not a dog. They are completely different." The orchard owner half a preacher helped dedicate him. All those who had known Silk and some who didn't took turns at the cold earth with spikes and shovels. The service was a couple minutes then everyone returned to work. Little Wallis stood atop Silk's grave and cried. Beans had never heard an animal cry before and she decided it was the worst thing she'd ever heard. When night hushed all the camp, Beans dried her eyes too and swore herself a new man. She would begin spinning her own tales at night. She would become somebody from out yonder and nobody from down south. Unseen behind the dancing fire licks stood a phantom bum in blue overalls. He saw to it with a goodnight dirge and went home.

In honor of their friend, Beans pointed to the night sky and whispered to little Wallis, "The stars–the principalities–also orphans, albeit their own faults–they always get a bit jealous of us and our brief season here. We are not pressed into the same pattern. It's maple leaves to bear for us–we know when it's time to move on."

TWO SOLDIERS

Daytime he's eighty-five. Nightime he's twenty. That's when he goes searching through those thin places for the boy who flipped his cap up, to keep him awake and alive on that long truck ride with no headlamps underneath the NKPA. He can tell me about friendly fire raining down he dove into a foxhole breaking his nose frozen ground bounced like putty under him. The order came down: stand or die. It was whoopty-doo already obvious boys after running tankards full of fuel up the mountainside under heavy fire at Pusan, smoking pall malls all the way up and down.

He remembers all this and more he doesn't say. But from the day after that trip with the boy who flipped his cap up, to keep him awake and alive to now sixty-five years later, he doesn't remember. Can't remember his face, his name what happened when he arrived what it was about, don't remember coming back, he repeats this play *He is on the road with a boy taking turns driving hanging a flashlight out the window down a frozen dirt road. The boy flipping his cap up, wake up.*

He said he chewed aspirin all the time, stood in a below-zero line watching boys throwing their medals back at their captain, medals are for the dead. He said he ate frozen turkey leftover from WWII for months. He watched Marilyn Monroe and Jane Bruner through the scope of his rifle. He felt a force-like wind touch his shoulder while praying. The boys cried the boys sang the boys went mad, he said. They eat sleep kill in revolutions like a county fair ride. Captain said if another shoots his foot he will get one in the head. You can't explain it there are no words for it staring down a dark road at a pace so slow it's confining and painful staying wake pert near impossible when the boy dozed off he'd reach over flip his cap up, wake up. No memory past that just a kid he never saw again.

He came home to an empty street. At a hole-in-the-wall card party, a guy asked if he'd been on vacation, the explanation cost two nights in the clink. He ran into a light pole on purpose outside Cantril drunk as an uncle henry. Then he found work and lots of it. Dark to dark with lots of PBR. Years later two brat kids and a beautiful but ornery wife. Running mail between townships, managing the dx station, coaching fast-pitch softball Selling seed corn, pushing dirt, and raising vegetables and a granddaughter. Not easy trying to squeeze life through a sieve and judging what comes through. Once the movement of the day stopped he needed to find that boy that flipped his cap up keeping him awake and alive, after paying dues everything coming and going being born while dying a little each day That last half of the phantom isn't too much to ask. Toward the end, he was laid upon scratchy hospital sheets A sacrifice of a life, a belly full of infection flooding him. He said a bodiless head with a familiar smirk floated above him. Hey, you sonofabitch, where the hell have you been? A ticket for the ferry and someone to ride it with. where they went is unknown but he left soon after with the boy who flipped his cap up to keep him awake and alive.

CATTYWAMPUS

Back when Christ was still a Corporal, she was here. Maggie moves back and forth all day long into the night the girl sees her clearly like now yet far away from home. She hears her and speaks her words through her own lips. *Straighten up and fly right,* she'd say, she'd sing. Maggie's lectures on pie crusts being too thick or thin. The girl would get a worried cussing between coffee breaks. Her poor decisions concerning snatchelbritches. *Sister, you didn't— but he had good insurance. Be still, my heart.* Then you marry him, the girl said. Rotary phone always ringing. Maggie'd call her up midnights asking if she was okay, *just a feeling,* she'd say, click.

The girl couldn't tell her about the tilted and crooked. Jesus, I'm fine, she'd say. *Don't sass,* and click. Maggie was right in a long linear way. The girl soon realizes good hurts worse than the bad. She smokes too much and gets lost in the night. *Quit your smoking, sister, click. Ah hell, I forgot what I was going to tell you, click. Ah hell, I remembered. Cover your flowers frosts coming,* click. Maggie's a decade gone, the phone is off the hook. The girl is living somewhere within the torn veil. A two-world walker. She haunts hallways and gravel roads. Too late to chat with Maggie too early for some kind of dawn.

SASSIE

Alma got drunk and drove to the first place along the road that looked like a forest. An hour before, she stumbled through Goodwill and bought a Sony Walkman with headphones and two cassettes. Sam Cooke and Tina Turner. It was too hot for May but when you are drunk enough you don't care that it's hotter than a peach orchard boar or you stink worse than one or your mascara streakings and this suggests to a very nosey stranger that you are a manic depressive and perhaps in need of prayer?

Lying on ant planet, she played her music and sang as loudly as possible. Youyouyouyousendme darling youyouyousendme darling youdoyoudo oh whoa oh woah. This might have gone on for hours. It was how she first met him. The singing might have sounded like a dying cow in a mudhole. Still, it worked somehow and he loved those songs he'd never heard. She dedicated each drunken ballad to Sassie. Thinking that somehow, this pernicious memory dream from twenty-eight years ago was actually real and not a phantasm of dissociative disorder. Certain smells produced authenticity. Wet dog and wet towels. Pine sweetness. She felt around, rummaging her fingers in the dirt, sticks and mossy bugs, and rotting wood. It all felt so goddamn good.

The canopy of leaves and streaming sunlight produced postcard sympathy card for a deceased loved one, an image beat the dead horse in the ground. Still. There is no denying the simple in-your-face beauty of it all, most especially when you're dead-on-your-ass drunk. It's easier to talk to God, that way, it's easier to scream and your long-dead parent's self-pity party is an all-nighter and at the nosy Church of God Priss who wanted to pray for you in the middle of a thrift store but not really for you, no, not really for you. What we do for the golden star chart.

If her Sassie didn't show this time and she woke up in the haze of a noonday, possibly a weekday, more than likely feeling stupid for the drinking part not the Sasquatch hunting part but that she is forty-two years old and cannot simply drink like a kid anymore and get away with it. She is dying to her fate but still somehow hopeful the next wild hair she gets to drive forty-five minutes to get a case of beer because she lives in a dry county, she will finally reunite with him and hopefully, Lord willing and the crick don't rise, be welcomed, invited, re-homed with him. This of course will all turn into a book. Drunken wet pages but it's the only way you can get back there or go in the first place.

PIZZA AND STEAKHOUSE STARS

The summer before I was a pinwheel pattern with four arms fresh out the Milky Way. I was washing dishes in a tiny ass backroom with the Keo bum Walt Whitman look-alike. Greek thin pizza crusts, ribeye fats, ketchup-covered fries. Scraping, rinsing oval plates with scorching hot water with a wall-mounted pull-down kitchen faucet. We were shoulder to shoulder and thigh to thigh. He didn't speak. The universe is still expanding outward, even here. One night and past 10 p.m. orders still coming in—Jesus christ, goddammit, sonofabitch, it's hotter than a peach orchard boar. He nodded. I scraped, rinsed. He washed dried stacked. Smoke break outside together looking up. "Every star you see has at least one planet," I explained. He nodded. Then a big puff and sigh. Keo bum dropped the t. "I went to prison for my brother— not for him but for mother. He'd have been killed. I don't hurt kids." Deep shaky low voice guttural truth there, goosebumps. Like a stray dog, I took him in. "When I grow up, I'm moving to the neighboring galaxy," I said. "It's called Andromeda."

REMEMBER

morning, memorial day. i lie still with hands crossed over my chest—holding my breath for as long as i can. granny hollers up the stairs to get around. i move stiff legs zombie stare practicing death. get a move she hollers and i croke like an old bull frog. she finishes her bite of toast a swallow of coffee. her white feathers combed out needs a new perm. i slurp soggy cornflakes—watch her from the window cutting hydrangeas and irises putting them in jars. i'm eleven years old, dying of a rare disease and soon i'll be getting flowers.

on the tan dash of the wagon reads *Malibu Classic*. i roll down windows for some air conditioning. we drive to cantril first. aunts uncles cousins buried there. i hear the jars clink louder going up cemetery hill. i met Paul here he used to roll his own cigarettes. he was a good man took care of granny like she was his own. the old woman is deep in memory—we're there a long while he's standing there—i think she's gone somewhere else.

she walks away quickly—she's mad—she gets mad when she cries. i decide not to tell her i'm dying today—i give away my handful of dandelions. i'm not mad at her anymore she is complicated she is a little girl.

four more cemeteries. and she will place her hand on each stone. we are quiet driving to visit the dead—my family—friends—my stories. everyone is seen in a sidemirror. i can look back without turning around the dead are more alive now than they ever were.

A SELF-CONTAINED PLANE OF EXISTENCE

A child was born at the old hospital in Burlington. Her mama's room window was open and a couple of stories below were the wide rolling waters of the Mississippi River. This child recalls moving water in the night and the smells of mud and milk. There are pictures of mama and a crinkly-pink-faced baby with a styrofoam cup taped to the top of her little head where the nurses kept the IV in place. This child's father flirted with the nurses and looked like a Sunday man to everyone around. Let me buy you a sandwich he tells somebody just in hopes they could or would love him. All his gifts were in the end too expensive. He would squeeze mama's hand so tight she cried when he didn't like what she was saying or doing.

If the child wanted to believe in something more, something chimerical–she was in trouble. It would be like walking past an injured puppy. Hide the light. Hide it away because he is always on the prowl looking for a heart valve to slit.

Birthdays and holidays are when her people don't tell the truth. The people came in and went out. She had a large scratchy teddy bear named Pinky. He couldn't help it and she held him anyway. The child's father hid her away and she tried to hold him too. This is a pattern in the child's stars. Did she dream about what was to come? She knew this story from before. Now, wherever that before is there's no map. The river in her muddy cells carried those beings of creation, the little brownie photographs, and family folklore–snagging along the way one word of a child standing out in the black like a single star in the dark. The child moves deadheads with the action of winds sending trash all around so she can slip through currents. Her name day is Mesopotamia a land between rivers. Before and after pleated into a vanishing point. Standing in the bottom land of silt, she could see at water level. If she knew the end it wouldn't matter much—soon enough she'll forget and birth the child again.

FLAT

It's long past the last supper and the rumbling skies echo in my belly where spirit rests. I don't have an umbrella and I don't want one. Lights up ahead. A grain truck rolls up to a slowing stop I wave a hand for him to go on. There's no gravel dust, I bless the spitting of the rain—an easy sprinkle, maybe she is trying to help. I can't walk right straight, kicking up rocks. Equilibrium fell off years ago. The feeling underfoot always makes me look down. I'm no longer pointed home. I look back through light rain to my car but I see his. The sky is annoyed with me—I'm a dawdler. Still out here holding things up. I holler at her grey breasts to *let her rip*. She does. A loud crack of thunder and a dim yellow flash give purple glows. I see up ahead a decrepit hay barn with a new light pole. there are only a few more farms till home. A realm can split easily without any fuss. There's a boy with short black hair and green eyes. I see a shabby reflection of him walking with me. I start to speak to him and stop. His rare smile formed like a little square above his chin. In the purple dark, in between lightning strikes, clouds hide the stars but they cannot hide me. Every whipstitch is the same farm lamp besides machine sheds and outbuildings. Old cracker box houses hunch and sigh.

I try to walk quickly and quietly past Jim Metcalf's cows. They low at me concerned like grandmothers. Through the fence are green reflective cow eyes. The air smells of manure and sweet grass. I look back and the car is gone, even in flashes of light, it is not there. Then she lets loose again but it's much colder. It rains hard for about two minutes and I only get a few feet further. Could be all night or another minute. Her breasts rest again. I am soaked through but still walking—a cramp tickles my side. This boy still walks beside me, looking at me for something. Up ahead I see a flickering candle inside my window. Walking faster, my wet jeans weigh heavy and chafe my inner thighs. I try to walk not think. Anything but everything. Green windows, and a square smile. Flat tires and stink bugs. Cottonseeds, they all were. A decade headache, such fluff, and blur, a colorless memory. I was trapped in that car for too damn long. Less than half an hour and I will be back under my quilt in dry clothes. I will forget about the muddy seeds matted in my hair for now. I'll lay a towel over my feather pillow and dream my prayers. I walk through grey puddles in the front drive, under the first lamp post. The mailman left the box door open again. I see Granny or a version of her telling me how lightning prefers Cottonwoods. There are so many down these gravel roads.

OLD HATS

one last time, down county roads. all headlights and buicks. she has forgotten lyrics, liars, warm beer cans. side table whitman, two lines, she slaps her face, pinches her thighs. a red plastic flashlight, the only light. *Suite Judy Blue Eyes* turned up louder. marmalade jam for her toast. homeless slippers for her feet. worn oak flooring, grainy coffee, the damn filters flooding again. orange sunrise morning, ringing lines, cold sausages, cast iron skillet. smell of moldy mothballs also liars. she slips into nightshade clothes. magnetic interference full tilt. plenty of old hats, and long fallen hairs.

before civil wars—full eyes, and poppycocks. her kin pickling in malice. hugs appearing gentle. notecards with bad clipart lily of the valley. shortest of stories. cut down to such a small thing. a three-paragraph life. the living just want the dead done. made up memories, maybe. shaded just so, forty-eight colors. clay heads and torsos, bronze legs, and feet. blood-borne dreams. liberty and ragged flags. tap trumps, american legion boys fire shots that clack the air. she picks up shells from the ground. the only son gets up to speak, tramples the grass carpet, talks about himself instead of his dead father.

fists full of iowa dirt and crabgrass. navy blue instead of black. aunt believing bible thumping hell is for her personal use. everyone unbuckles. breathes easier, lowing chatter, senior center serves fruit punch seven-up. she shakes the dust from her own feet. gravel parking lot, it's hers alone. she smokes a lot, and cloud watches. eats a pulled pork sandwich side of noodle salad. she talks to god by herself.

GILLS 1992, GRANNY'S VERSION

this time, the air was just right. warm on cool, a yellow-green film right before a genuine gulleyworsher. a fat toad-soaker of a storm. minty, a motherless wonder ten-year-old wild woman of borney oaks. bread and gravy she'd say is a modicum of respect among her folks. a gal ghost of the Greenbrae clan. she was a bit cut down from life. forlorn for loss always a quarter store. black trunks old gray tee. she left the vestibule of ages in style. she jumped from the savanna-sabula bridge into the mighty miss with a prayer request reverse. a jonah—to be swallowed by a giant catfish. the Good Lord consented.so the mud divided itself—split wide apart in the bosky dells. this s a well-known ballad throughout the boonies. on chicken-peck backroads behind mossy limestone walls, she stayed with him until her eighties like all cordial mortals, dancehall dandies. she floated on a calcite sheet into the gulf. a blue heron passed over. her soul was translated into water. a quiet ceremonious surrender.

IDOLONS

every other damn night I am back at 211 Market Street. even though the white stucco house is stripped of her flowers–the white hydrangeous, the irises, the little red tea roses climbing the arbor—and they changed the fucking tin roof from green to blue which looks like shit. I am there in my mind but worse i'm deeper than any memory i have ever known. they are alive in it and it's so goddamn real. I open the screendoor into the back porch and Jim is wagging his black tail christ he got fat as a tick. Pappy still gives him frozen hot dogs.I twist the glass knob of the old door and open it to the smell of bacon. He's gonna make me some bacon sammiches with toast and grape jelly. granny is in the living room recliner and you can hear dr. phil get turned way down so she can hear what's going on in the kitchen. I smell her. she's got a new perm. what the hell's going on, he jabs at me. he likes to pick at me and I like to pick back at him. don't burn it too goddamn much. he is the burner of all things good–like poor man's steak and grilled cheese. she is the measurer of fabric and flours. I can't let go of these things. all that is measured, sewn, and burned into my mind and to say, this is not real. but it is. someone tell me this is not real. someone, please pull back my lids and pour in something else.

HEY VANCE

River clams are talking these days. Fishnet Willie Jefferson says so and that he's no man at all—meaning he ain't human. His neck radio plays mostly static but he says they are sirens singing from the Ouachita. I don't believe much of what anybody says these days but I'll listen to his river clams. But still, Fishnet Willie Jefferson says he's no man at all—meaning he's above man. Hey Vance, do you believe it? This is a cloudy afternoon back porch kind of talk. I know what you'll say, Vance, that this fella is a human and probably a man but I still want to hear it and watch your face when you say it. Fishnet is back on his corner bucket again today with his talking clams. I'll drive the back roads with you clear to Texarkana if you'll call me and talk about it.

SONGS FROM THE BACKYARD

It was hot for early summer. The kind of heat that makes your eyesight blurry, and your second change of clothes damp before you step outside of the house. It's too hot for words. It was June and the grass was yellow. We were preparing for a get-together. Granny set the tea out in the sun next to the grill. The white strings of the tea bags were trapped under the clenched lid of the jar. The tags flittered and danced to the wave of the warm breeze. Three rickety lawn chairs sat empty alongside of the house. Then a little sound ushered in something new.

White noise and scratches, skips of a record–the humdrum of one o'clock in the afternoon changed into a soothing rhythm. Welcome Billie, have a seat. "Don't mind if I do." Before we knew it the people started roaming in. It seems as though they were coming here just for her. Damn if she doesn't make you wish for rain to ruin the barbecue. Pennies from Heaven falling down, hitting the poor senseless folks who wouldn't know good soul from a wormhole in the ground. And they forgot something. But don't you remember? She said, make sure your umbrella's upside down and we were really listening–you bet your life we were.

Young and old lined themselves up to get some red ribs on their paper plates. There was a pyramid of golden corn on the picnic table right in front of Uncle Deacon. His light blue eyes reflected all the happy and the sad. When he was a boy he could eat two whole watermelons. Billie knows. She's got the old kind of wisdom. God bless the child that's got his own...that's got his own.

You and I used to sit in those lawn chairs against the house. We would always wait til Aunt Dallas brought us our plates. We couldn't miss a note or a soul walking by, fanning themselves and exclaiming that it was "hotter than a peach orchard boar." Someone would holler about the water and it would be turned on. The kids would jump through and scream but not one of those yahoos could drown her out. Sometimes a kid would sing her words. "Who do you think is coming to town, you'll never guess who...We would look at each other and smile. That kid got it. Loveable, huggable, Miss Emily Brown. Miss Brown to you.

Just as the sun started tipping its hat over that oak trip, the old folks would start yawning and the kids would lie about the grass with their arms and legs stretched out in exhaustion. Pappy would start talking about seed corn. It was time to go. We never moved an inch and we watched them shuffle back out. Bille sounded sad. Gloomy Sunday. The tea jar was empty and so was the yard. We sat there til dark and chewed on blades of grass. We looked up into the dark blues of the sky. We sang with her then. Summertime and the living is easy. No one was there to listen to our sour notes. She took that sweet gentle pitch of hers and glazed it over the top of our little heads. On the backs of fireflies, we would try to catch up but we could barely hold on to her skirt as she turned around and around under the stars. Only Billie could fly.

Sal Ragen is a neurodivergent poet and fiction writer. She is a self-described river rat from Southeast Iowa having lived in so many river towns over the years. She can often be found out on the water in a jon boat with a typewriter. Her love for stories was instilled by her grandma Maggie who would recite *Little Orphan Annie* by memory at bedtime. She was also inspired by her Pappy who often told her local legends while driving around Van Buren County, Iowa.

Currently, she's an MFA candidate at the University of Nebraska-Omaha and is set to graduate in January 2024. She will be a student for life and you may find her future eighty-year-old self still taking creative writing classes. Sal is the recipient of an Academy of American Poets University Prize and her work has appeared or is forthcoming in *Dogwood, Allegory Ridge: Aurora, River Heron Review, Pine Row, The MacGuffin, Spectrum Literary Journal,* and *Red Coyote*. She currently lives in the Ouachita mountains with her husband and large fur family. She is at work on a novel.